Basic Principles For Growing Churches

Accounting And Administrative
Guidelines That Promote
Church Growth

Arnold Cirtin, CPA

CSS Publishing Company, Inc., Lima, Ohio

BASIC BUSINESS PRINCIPLES FOR GROWING CHURCHES

Library of Congress Cataloging-in-Publication Data

Cirtin, Arnold, 1931-
   Basic business principles for growing churches : accounting and administrative guidelines that promote church growth / Arnold Cirtin.
      p. cm.
   ISBN 0-7880-2415-9 (perfect bound : alk. paper)
   1. Church finance. 2. Church management. I. Title.
   BV770.C56 2006
   254—dc22

                                                                    2005034439

For more information about CSS Publishing Company resources, visit our website at www.csspub.com or email us at custserv@csspub.com or call (800) 241-4056.

Cover designed by Barbara Spencer
ISBN 0-7880-2415-9   PRINTED IN U.S.A.

To my lovely wife,
Betty

Table Of Contents

Author's Preface

I am first and foremost a teacher, and this is a teaching book. Its purpose is to show pastors of small and medium sized churches how to successfully administer the affairs of their organizations. Note that I did not include pastors of large churches in this list. There is a high probability that they have already learned how or their churches would not have become large. Of course, this book is not intended only for pastors. Treasurers and other board members will also find it useful.

Success may seem an inappropriate term for an ecclesiastical discussion. This wording is often associated with personal ambition, professional achievement, and individual affluence. Perhaps, but the opposite of success is failure, and we cannot find support for failure anywhere in the Bible. Christians are not exhorted to strive for it. On the other hand, a strong argument can be made that biblical inspiration encourages success. Accordingly, Christians have been given the right to choose between success and failure. Success is better.

It is necessary to address a couple of conventions of English usage. Ours is a rich language. Sir Winston Churchill described the English sentence as "a noble thing." However, for all its power and beauty, English does not have an acceptable neuter personal pronoun. With an exception or two, *it* will not do when referring to human beings. It has always been accepted English practice to use the masculine pronoun when the sex of the person is not known. This is known as a synecdoche, a figure of speech in which a part stands for the whole.

William F. Buckley, Jr., has provided us with two examples: "He who laughs last laughs best." Does this mean that *she* who laughs first laughs best, or that laughing last is better? "Man's inhumanity to man." Does this mean that men are inhumane to other men but humane to women, or that people have been known to be inhumane to each other? These examples show the synecdoche at work.

I taught a federal income tax course in which I used an outstanding textbook. However, its entire narrative was sprinkled with "he or she," "him or her," and "his or hers." After two or three chapters of this I began to get the impression that we have two sexes — but I already knew that. What I needed to know was something about income tax. These double-barreled pronouns became a distraction, and they actually obscured what the author was trying to teach. I prefer conventional English usage, for it is better to be grammatically correct than politically correct.

The other convention concerns first, second, and third person pronouns. Except for mystery novels, the majority of books are written in the third person. This book follows this practice with the occasional use of the second person to enhance the conversational tone. As a practicing accountant I have a wealth of experience, which I frequently draw upon to illustrate important points. In such cases I use the first person pronouns *I*, *me*, and *my*. Thus it is possible to avoid such cumbersome phrases as "The author found that ..." and "The pastor met with the author...." The infrequent appearance of first person pronouns in relating actual experience makes for easier reading.

As a teenage Christian, I wanted to be a minister. The Lord, in his wisdom, did not call me to that vocation. (There are probably some thankful congregations out there somewhere.) Teaching in a secular university became my calling, and writing this book is part of that ministry.

Arnold Cirtin, A.B., M.B.A., Ph.D., CPA

Chapter I

Business Principles In Church? Amen!

In any meeting of a group of Christians, particularly Christian men, it is common for one of them to make a statement something like this: "A church is not a business and should not be run like a business."

What are we to make of such a statement? It is easy to imagine several responses. "Amen, Brother!" "Right on!" "That's true. Business principles have no place in church!" These comments are usually accompanied by knowing nods of the head.

It is not difficult to see the well-meaning reasoning behind this perception. After all, the business world is one thing; the church is something else. It is different, set apart. Although business principles are generally recognized as useful and efficient, the reputation of business does not enjoy high marks, primarily because of movies and television. The church, being sacred, is above the grubby practices employed in business. The goal of business is profit, while the mission of the church is something else, but certainly not profit.

These reactions and others like them fall short of the mark. Here is a better answer to those negative perceptions: "Why not? Why shouldn't a church be run like a business?"

Why not, indeed. What happens when a church is run like a business? What does a church gain when it uses business principles in its operations? It gets the advantages of accountability, communication of financial results, fiscal responsibility, efficient management, stewardship of God's resources, and internal control. You will notice that there is nothing among these advantages that is inconsistent with the Christian message.

What are the disadvantages of using business principles in administering the affairs of the church? If there are any, they are extremely difficult to identify.

It is true that one of the goals of business is to earn a profit. All successful businesses have many other objectives, such as good corporate citizenship, responsibility in the community, well-being of employees, high quality of products, and protection of the environment, but profit must remain a major goal. This is because, without profits, a company cannot continue in business. It must have profits to survive. A company that consistently loses money will eventually go out of business. We all know of many fine business organizations that no longer exist. This is because they failed to earn profits and instead accumulated losses.

The Nature Of Profit

There are those who have a very dim view of profit. They consider profit as being bad, and they describe profit as money-grubbing, obscene, even pornographic. Let's consider the logic of these views. If profits are bad, then losses must be good. It can't be any other way. But it must be good for companies to remain in business, producing needed goods and services, and providing jobs for the community. Conversely, it is always bad news when a company goes out of business. Its production is lost to society, less money is added to the economy, and jobs are lost. When looked at in this way, profits are not only necessary, they are good. George Gilder has correctly pointed out that business organizations are actually altruistic in outlook. They invest vast amounts of capital at considerable risk in the hope of making a profit, which is by no means certain. Such altruism benefits many segments of the economy, and it may benefit the corporation, its management, and its stockholders. Then again, it may not. We know that some businesses fail, and both they and society are the losers.

Here is an incontrovertible fact. A company that makes a profit adds more value to society than it takes out. The opposite is also true. A company that suffers losses removes more value from society than it puts in. There is no way that this can be good for society.

What is profit? Its definition is simple. Profit is revenues in excess of expenses. In general, revenues are sales. In an accounting firm or a doctor's office, revenues are called fees, and in a real estate agency they are called commissions. In a merchandising company they are simply called sales. In any event, they represent the sale of goods and services. Expenses are the costs of doing business. When revenues exceed expenses a profit happens. Conversely, when expenses are greater than revenues a loss is incurred.

By definition, nonprofit organizations do not make profits. This is certainly true, but only in a technical sense. Even churches must have revenues greater than expenses, because any church which does not take in more than it spends will not be able to accomplish its mission. We can conclude, then, that one characteristic of a church when compared to a business is that the excess of revenues over expenses is not called profit.

Should We Or Shouldn't We?

All of this suggests that, in order to assure that the church has sufficient revenue to cover its expenses, perhaps it should be run like a business. It is healthy for those in church administration to never think in terms of profit-making, but it is equally healthy to never forget the necessity of keeping expenses less than revenues.

Should a church be run like a business? Let's ignore this question for a moment and consider the proposition that the church is a business, and in some communities it is one of the most prominent businesses in town. It purchases real estate, constructs buildings, buys massive amounts of furnishings and equipment, hires personnel, pays salaries and wages, withholds payroll taxes and other deductions, and performs the same functions as other businesses. The pastor is the president of a corporation and in some cases chairman of the board. There is no question, then, that when business principles are employed, the church benefits.

However, it is healthy to think of the church as something other than a business, as something greater, existing on a higher plane. The church must be thought of as something special, even sacred, ordained by God and filled with his Spirit. For this reason, God deserves the best that we have to offer. We can't do better than to provide the church with accountability, communication of financial information, fiscal responsibility, efficient management, stewardship of God's resources, and internal control.

11

Accountability

This concept is closely associated with church governance. There are two types of church governance, episcopal and presbyterian, and both require accountability. Episcopal simply means that the organization has bishops, and the episcopal form of governance is from the top down. Authority and responsibility flow in a downward direction. Presbyterian means that the organization has presbyters, and this form of governance is from the bottom up. Authority and responsibility flow in an upward direction. In both types of organization, everyone is accountable to someone else. In successful businesses, the lines of authority and responsibility are well defined. For example, the controller reports to the vice president of finance, and the vice president reports to the president. In churches these lines of authority are often blurred. For example, do maintenance personnel report to the pastor or to the board of trustees? Does the associate pastor have executive responsibility when the pastor is away? These and other questions of accountability need to be considered and put into practice. It is just as important for a successful church to utilize the concept of accountability as it is for a successful business.

Communication Of Financial Results

In many churches, preparing financial reports for the monthly board meeting is a plague visited on the treasurer and office staff. Making financial statements for the annual business meeting is even worse. There is never enough time to get them done, they are usually barely completed in time for the meeting, and as a result they are often poorly done. The main thing is, "We got them out." The fact that they do not communicate as well as they should is overlooked. After all, what do you expect given the time constraints? Yet businesses routinely prepare financial statements every month, they are provided to management early in the month, and they communicate the desired information that management needs. Why is this? It is because they use business principles in preparing their financial reports, and their accounting systems are designed with that result in mind. Churches should do the same.

Here is a case history from my own experience. A large and successful church in a major city was experiencing difficulty in getting its accounting work completed in a timely manner, including monthly and annual financial reporting. It had a wonderful bookkeeper hired to work three days a week. She was actually working four days a week and couldn't get the work done. The monthly board meeting was a major chore and the annual business meeting was a nightmare for her. This was because the financial reports were compiled from information scattered throughout the books and files with no rational organization. The job was massive and frustrating.

I examined the chart of accounts and changed it to contain numerical consistency. Then I redesigned the books so that recorded transactions would flow into the financial statements. This made periodic reporting a copy job rather than a gathering of disparate information. A difficult job became easy. The result was that the bookkeeper resumed her three day per week schedule, she easily met her reporting deadlines, and she had time on her hands.

By now you will have observed that the key to efficient communication of financial results is based on the accounting system. That is why there is a chapter on accounting in this book.

Fiscal Responsibility

Whose money is it, anyway? God's? The church's? The congregation's? Whatever the answer, it is clear that those who spend it have considerable responsibility to do it properly.

Corporate officers are subject to the business principle that they are responsible for the funds entrusted to them by stockholders, customers, and lenders. The company's success depends upon how well they discharge that responsibility. Church officers have the same obligation to their parishioners that corporate officers have to their stockholders. Regardless of whose money it is, the fact is that the pastor and the board did not produce the income. This was provided by the individual members of the congregation in meeting their commitments to God. This should not be taken lightly, and pastors and board members should never forget this basic truth.

Fiscal responsibility is closely associated with financial reporting. A fair question is, "How much should be reported?" The general rule is the more the better. Church members can usually be trusted to use financial information responsibly. Church officers are sometimes reluctant to be candid when reporting financial information to their congregations. The thinking is that some items are too sensitive to be reported in detail. An interesting example is a line item on the financial statement of a large church that read, "Maintenance and salaries." This was a large dollar amount that contained no information about either salaries or maintenance. Apparently, the pastor's salary was too sensitive to be disclosed to the people who paid it.

The church has a responsibility to be honest and open with its members. Look at the financial reports of any publicly held corporation. They provide massive amounts of financial data for anyone who wants it, including stockholders, of course, but also employees, labor unions, the government, and their competitors. Look at their proxy statements and you will find salaries, bonuses, and stock options of the officers. Are corporations less sensitive about these things than churches? Not at all. Should churches provide complete financial information in their reporting? They would be better off if they did.

This discussion is apt to make some pastors and board members nervous. The cure for this nervousness is to begin to open up and provide more information in the financial statements. This will benefit the congregation and they will appreciate the trust exhibited by their leadership.

Efficient Management

We have all read that one of the major causes of business failure is poor management. The corollary is also true — good management breeds success.

Management is both an art and a science. Like all the arts it is inherited; some people are born with it and some are not. And like all sciences it is cognitive; people can learn it. Those who are born with it have an advantage, but even they can benefit from learning.

The good news is that those who are not so endowed can become very effective managers through learning.

If effective management is necessary for business success, it follows that churches can also benefit from it. Look at any successful church and you will find that good managers are in charge. It is usually not called management, but it is present in every church that has excellent leadership.

How does one learn management skills? There are many management text books, and they can be found in libraries and bookstores everywhere. They sometimes contain a lot of boring detail, so if you go in this direction be quite selective in your reading. Read only those topics that are useful and interesting to you.

Stewardship Of God's Resources

Do we need to discuss this subject? Actually we already have. Our discussion of accountability, communication of financial results, fiscal responsibility, efficient management, and internal control is a discussion of outstanding stewardship. As we earnestly work toward the accomplishment of these goals, good stewardship is inevitable.

The resources that come into the church are usually from two sources, contributions and loans. The point is that this is someone else's money. It does not belong to the pastoral staff or the board, but these groups have responsibility for properly using the funds entrusted to them. Responsibility and stewardship are closely related.

What will be the end result of applying business principles in doing the church's business? There are two. The congregation will be satisfied with the quality of its leadership, and the church will grow in size and influence. Small churches will become medium sized, and medium sized churches will become large.

Is size important? Not really. Large churches became large for a reason and small churches remain small for a reason. Although size is not important, growth is. Among other things, a growing church provides evidence that it is meeting the spiritual needs of a great many people, and that is very important.

Chapter 2

Internal Control, The Safety Net

Internal control is not a household term. Most people have never heard of it, although it is probably the most important principle in every business. We never get done talking about it.

Every company whose stock is traded in the financial markets must be audited by a firm of certified public accountants, and the audited financial statements must be filed with the Securities and Exchange Commission. The first step in the audit is to make a study and evaluation of internal control. The scope of the remainder of the audit depends on the efficacy of the company's internal control system. Good internal control means less auditing, and poor internal control means more auditing. In some cases, internal control is so lacking that an audit cannot be conducted. Since auditing by CPAs is very expensive, there are economic incentives for companies to have good internal control. It is even ensconced in federal law. The Racketeer-Influenced and Corrupt Organizations (RICO) Act requires, among other things, that every traded company must maintain an internal control system. There are many good reasons for effective internal control. It is simply good business, and all successful organizations have excellent internal control.

The point is that, although internal control is not widely discussed among the general public, few things are more important in the operation of a business. This is equally true for churches. Here is not only a description of internal control but also guidance on how to install this needed system in your church.

What is internal control? There are four parts.

- Protection of assets
- Reliability of accounting records
- Operational efficiency
- Adherence to the organization's policies

The first two are accounting controls and the last two are administrative controls. We are going to concentrate on the first two, the accounting controls.

The First Accounting Control

When we think of protecting assets we have all assets in mind, including cash, supplies, inventory, and equipment. Although we are interested in all assets, our emphasis has to be on cash. The reasons are obvious. Cash is high in value, low in bulk, and its ownership cannot be traced. Accordingly, a major part of our internal control effort is concentrated upon cash.

Most churches have already given some thought to internal control of cash. This is represented by the use of two signature checks. The treasurer writes and signs the checks and another board member, usually the secretary, countersigns them. The logic is that the requirement of a second signature prohibits any abuses that are possible with one signature. In practice, it is sometimes difficult to get the second signature in order to meet the church's obligations in a timely manner. Secretaries have been known to sign a stack of checks in advance to enable the treasurer to perform his duties easily, and of course this reduces the process to a single signature check. There goes internal control. There is a better way. With proper internal control, a church can safeguard its cash and safely revert to one signature checks.

There are two requirements for the internal control of cash:

1. There must be a separation of duties such that the person who has custody of cash does not do any bookkeeping for cash, and the one who does the bookkeeping does not have access to cash.
2. All cash receipts must be deposited intact and all bills must be paid by check.

Requirement 1

In a large office, separation of duties is easy, but not automatic. It is common for office procedures to inadvertently violate this requirement. In small offices separation of duties is difficult. One

18

person often acts as receptionist, secretary, mail clerk, and bookkeeper. As mail clerk, this individual receives incoming checks and makes the bank deposit. As bookkeeper, the same individual records cash receipts, writes the checks, and records them. In this situation there is no effective internal control. Can this problem be solved? Yes, but it is necessary to take imaginative action. At the very least, the pastor must be brought into the picture. Each month, a bank reconciliation must be prepared. In a small business where there is no separation of duties, the owner should reconcile the bank account. In a small church with a similar staffing situation, the pastor should. This will provide for some separation of duties which will strengthen internal control over cash. To be effective, the bank reconciliation must be done as soon as possible after the bank statement is received, no later than the next day. Delayed bank reconciliations leave the church vulnerable to misappropriation.

The good news is that this is an easy task for the pastor to perform, and it has the added benefit of involving him in the financial operation of the church. As the church grows, the office staff will need to be increased, and separation of duties can be instituted. At that time the pastor can retire from his bank reconciliation job.

Bank statements have a reconciliation form on the reverse side. Although the bank reconciliation can be made on plain paper, the best place to do it is on this valuable form. Incidentally, all businesses and churches, unlike individuals, should insist that their bank statements be prepared and mailed as of the last day of the month. This is necessary for financial statements, which are prepared as of the last day of the month, to reflect the true balance of cash.

Another internal control opportunity is available. In many churches the treasurer takes custody of cash receipts, makes the deposits, writes the checks, and does the bookkeeping. The separation of duties rule can be implemented by having the church secretary do the bookkeeping. Most treasurers would gladly welcome this sharing of responsibility.

Another internal control procedure for churches is the cash count ticket. This is a small form with an original and one or two copies, and it is filled out by the ushers after the offerings are taken.

In churches, cash receipts consist of checks, currency, and coins. The cash count ticket provides a systematic method for counting the cash, but there is an additional benefit. At least two of the ushers must sign the form to verify the accuracy of the count. One copy is given to the treasurer, one is filed in the church office, and the third copy, if any, can be kept by the head usher. These forms are available in some of the larger Christian bookstores and in mail order catalogs of church supply companies. An example is: Gospel Publishing House at 1-800-641-4310, item number 075371.

All checks written on the church bank account should be backed up with proper authorization. Invoices, receipts, and cash register tapes can provide the necessary evidence of authenticity. Check numbers should be written on them for cross referencing. Expenditures for which there is no documentary evidence can be backed up by an authorization voucher signed by someone in responsibility, such as the pastor.

Why is there such an emphasis on separation of duties? In all reported embezzlement cases, the common element is the lack of separation of duties. In order to remove cash, the embezzler must conceal the shortage by manipulating the records. There is no other way. Access to the cash and the accounting system is an absolute necessity for an embezzler to be successful. Separate the custody of the cash from the record keeping for cash and the possibility of embezzlement is greatly diminished.

Why all this discussion about embezzlement? Aren't we talking about Christians? Christians do not steal or lie or cheat. This is certainly true; Christians are not dishonest. But internal control is not about honesty, it is about good business. Its purpose is not to keep people honest; they are already honest. Internal control is simply the only acceptable way of doing business, and it must be employed in all organizations. What do you do when you find a dishonest employee? Improve internal control? Absolutely not. The correct approach is to politely tell him to clean out his desk as soon as possible and his final check will be ready for him at that time. There is no place in any organization for dishonesty, and no organization, including churches, can do without internal control.

Requirement 2

This procedure, to deposit all cash receipts intact and to pay all bills by check, is often violated in everyday practice. This simply means that 100% of the cash coming in is taken to the bank. It also means that bills are paid with checks, not with some of the cash that has been collected. You have probably been in small businesses when a delivery or a collect freight bill is paid out of the cash register. The cash register contains cash receipts, and they are being used to pay bills. This violates the rule, and internal control is seriously impaired.

Why is this so important? This is because the company, or church, has an outside agency, the bank, that keeps a record of all cash transactions, both receipts and payments. If all of the cash receipts are deposited, then the bank's record of deposits coincides with the church's actual receipts. If all bills are paid by check, the bank's record of disbursements equals the church's actual payments. If bills are paid from cash receipts there is no correspondence between the church's accounting and the bank's records.

This equality between the bank's and the church's record keeping exists over time, but from one month to another there is a time lag. Cash receipts for the last day of the month will appear on the next month's bank statement, as well as the checks written during the last few days of the month. This time lag is solved by the bank reconciliation. For this reason the bank reconciliation is an important part of the internal control system. When the records of an outside entity, the bank, agree with the church's records, internal control is strong. The bank reconciliation provides evidence of this strength, especially if it is prepared by someone other than the one who has custody of the cash and the accounting system.

There may be a problem with this second requirement of paying all bills by check. There are times when ready cash is required. For example, the delivery truck driver and the collect freight bill must be paid immediately, and getting a check written and signed in a timely basis is sometimes hard to do. We need a fund of ready cash for these types of transactions. A petty cash fund is the answer.

Petty Cash

A petty cash fund is easily established. Determine approximately how much cash will be needed in the next four to five weeks. If you are uncertain of the needed amount, estimate $100 and write a check for that amount payable to Cash. Petty Cash is not an expense; it is another cash account. Note that the amount of the cash remains the same; it is now contained in two accounts instead of one.

Take the check to the bank and cash it. When the teller asks what you want, don't say, "Five twenties will do." Five twenties will not do. What you need is a roll of quarters, a roll of dimes, a roll of nickels, two rolls of pennies, and no rolls of half dollars. A half dollar will not do anything that two quarters will not do. You will need some ones, some fives, some tens, and no twenties. Bring the cash back to the office and place it in a useful container. Petty cash has been kept in manila envelopes, paper bags, cloth bags with a rubber band around the top, and cigar boxes. Although these containers work, after a fashion, the best place to keep it is in a petty cash box. These are available in office supply stores, of course, and at many discount stores. A petty cash box has a handle on top, a key lock in front, a coin and currency tray inside, and a compartment below the tray. There are several sizes of cash boxes, some quite large, but a petty cash box is smaller, approximately 11" x 8" x 4".

The rule for operating a petty cash fund is that you don't take any cash out unless you put something else in. When money is paid to the delivery truck driver or for any other purpose, you place the bill, invoice, cash register tape, or other documentation in the lower compartment. The best type of documentation for this purpose is the petty cash receipt. The bill, invoice, or cash register tape should be stapled to it. Pads of petty cash receipts are available in office supply stores, but not at discount stores. They are inexpensive and easy to use.

Eventually, the cash is going to run low and must be replenished. When this occurs, count the cash and the receipts. The total should be $100. Write a check payable to Cash in the exact amount of the receipts. This reimbursement check not only replenishes the petty cash fund, but it makes it possible to record in the books the expenses for which the cash was spent.

It is not unusual for the total of cash and receipts to be more or less than $100. The shortage or overage must be included in the amount of the reimbursement check. The account, Cash Short and Over, is used to account for the difference, if any.

In this manner, a petty cash fund fits into the internal control system. Though some expenditures are paid with cash, they eventually show up in a petty cash reimbursement check, thereby maintaining the requirement that all bills are paid by check.

By completely following these instructions the church will have good internal control of cash, and this important asset will be protected so it can be used in the Lord's valuable work.

The Second Accounting Control

It seems that everyone would be in favor of reliable records, so why make an issue of it? Actually, in this context, reliability of records has a technical connotation. Remember that auditors must make a study and evaluation of the internal control system, and one thing they do is determine how reliable the records are. Auditors cannot examine every transaction. It took a year to make those transactions, so how long would it take to examine them? About a year. Auditing consists of sampling and testing, and for this reason the auditors must be able to rely on the records. Even if an organization does not require an audit, reliable records are absolutely essential for efficient operation and financial reporting. A properly functioning internal control system provides this level of reliability.

For a church, an example of reliability of records would consist of the ledger being in balance and the bank reconciliation being in agreement with the cash account in the ledger and the checkbook.

Chapter 3

The Business Disciplines

Which is the most important? The major business disciplines we will discuss are accounting, finance, management, marketing, and production. Accounting is first in this alphabetical listing, so perhaps it is also the most important. Many people think so, especially accountants. These disciplines correspond roughly to the various departments in schools of business and the majors available to the students enrolled in them. Economics, business education, and quantitative analysis are also offered by many business schools, but they do not have much application in church administration.

Actually, accounting is not the most important. It is not even second in importance. The most important is marketing. Let's look at this from a business perspective, and then we can apply it to churches. If a company can solve its marketing problem, it can solve all of its business problems. It can buy all the accountants it wants. If the organization does not solve its marketing problem, it will have a hard time solving any of its other problems, or even continuing in existence. The accountants cannot help in such a situation. A business must sell its products and services in order to survive. If it fails to do so, no amount of management, production, finance, or accounting can provide success.

Second in importance, is production. If you can't make it, you can't sell it. The company's products must be produced in the quantity and quality desired by its customers so that the marketers can sell them.

Actually, accounting is third in importance. This is not to say that it and the other business activities fade to insignificance when compared to marketing. In fact, they are all indispensable to the functioning of a business because they are all interrelated. No activity is completely separate from the others. They complement each other and work together toward accomplishing the organization's goals.

As an example, let's look at production. Its importance in the hierarchy has already been established, but it needs accounting to see that the bills are paid and the production employees receive their paychecks. Without these and all other accounting functions, the production process could not continue. The same is true of the other departments, such as finance and management. They all contribute to one another's success, and each one needs the services of the others.

Do these business concerns relate to the administration of a church? The answer is a resounding "Yes!"

In this book more space is devoted to accounting than the other subjects. This is because accounting is the most technical of the business disciplines. It is the technical aspects of accounting that make life challenging for those who study it, as well as for the church treasurer. Because it is intertwined with everything else in church administration, if we do it right we are well on our way to doing everything else right.

Now let's look at the situation from the church's perspective. All five of the business activities come under the heading of church administration, and if done well they will improve the level of success by which the church accomplishes its divine mission. Administrative efficiency is enhanced when these activities are coordinated with one another. It is exciting when we think of church administration in connection with the church's mission of salvation of souls, meeting the spiritual needs of the congregation, disseminating the Word of God in the community and throughout the world, and all the other worthy goals that only the church is capable of accomplishing.

We can conclude, then, that all business functions are important because each one contributes to the mission of the organization. This is certainly true for the church organization. The purpose of this book is to enable pastors, staff, and board members to employ business principles in successfully accomplishing what God has called them to do.

The following chapters contain a detailed treatise on each of the five major business functions. By incorporating the tenets presented in these chapters, the church staff will be able to effectively use business principles in administering their church's affairs for the dissemination of the gospel and the furtherance of God's kingdom.

Chapter 4

Accounting, The Bean Counter's Art

Accounting intimidates people. It is technical, of course, and the widespread conception is that it requires a high level of mathematical ability. Accountants are regarded as talented mathematicians, and those whose math skills are somewhat rusty naturally feel intimidated.

The fact is, accountants are not mathematicians. They may know geometry, trigonometry, and calculus, but they do not use them in their work. Primarily, they use arithmetic. Occasionally, they use some elementary algebra, and auditors use statistical sampling, but arithmetic is the mathematical tool they use most. They are very good at addition, subtraction, multiplication, and division. They handle fractions well, but remember that fractions are fifth-grade technology. They manage decimals well also, and this is sixth-grade technology. They often make calculations mentally and come up with the right answers quickly. They can use a printing calculator for hours without ever looking at it; the touch system is natural for them, but none of this qualifies them as mathematicians. If you are hesitant in approaching accounting because it is mathematical, forget it. Everyone has had grade school arithmetic, so there is no reason to be intimidated. The proper attitude is to have confidence in your ability, and you should consider your ability equal to the task. Actually, accounting is a very logical and interesting process, and it is normal to have fun working with it. That, indeed, is the mindset you should have in approaching it.

In a church, accounting presides over two challenging chores, the financial report for the monthly board meetings and the financial statements for the annual business meeting. It is the rare church treasurer who would not affirm the massiveness of these tasks, but with an effective accounting system they are only minor challenges to be disposed of with dispatch. With such a system in place, reporting problems are solved at the beginning of the process, the design stage, so that the end of the process, the financial reporting stage, is nothing more than a copy job. This is the benefit of an effective accounting system, and there is no reason to have any other kind.

It is surprising how easy it is to have a well-performing accounting system. It is not necessary to know complex definitions or to have a large vocabulary of technical terms. The simple approach is available, and it is better than any other.

Two Methods Of Accounting

The cash basis and the accrual basis are both widely used. The cash basis is simpler and quite acceptable for church accounting. The reason it is easy is because it simply accounts for the cash coming in and the cash going out. Most cash comes in through offerings and are documented by cash count tickets and deposit slips. Cash goes out by writing checks, and these are backed up by invoices, receipts, and other documents. Tracking the inflow and outflow of cash is a fairly simple procedure. The accounting is complete when we record the source of the income — where the cash came from, and the expenses — what the money was spent for.

To make our discourse on accounting complete, let's discuss the accrual basis. Unlike the cash basis, revenue is recorded when it is earned rather than when it is received, and expenses are recorded when they occur rather than when they are paid. For example, in most businesses a sale is recorded when the service is completed or the merchandise is delivered, not when the cash is received later, usually in about thirty days. Similarly, an expense is recorded when it is incurred, not when it is paid about thirty days later. For this reason, this method requires two additional accounting books, one to record sales on credit and the related accounts receivable, and the other to record purchases on credit and the related accounts payable. The accrual basis is required for merchandising businesses and other medium-sized and larger firms, but it is unlikely that there are many churches using it. If a church finds it advisable to change from the cash to the accrual basis, it can be done, but it would require the services of a professional accountant. Therefore, we can forget about the accrual basis of accounting for our purposes. The cash basis will be quite satisfactory.

Manual Accounting Systems

Accounting requires bookkeeping, and there are two types of books used in accounting: They are journals and ledgers. Journals are used to record the daily transactions. The name comes from the French word, *jour*, meaning "day." We need a cash receipts journal to record the incoming cash, and a cash payments journal to record the outgoing cash. In all organizations there are a few transactions that do not involve cash. For this purpose we need a third journal, known as the general journal, to record these infrequent non-cash transactions.

Bookkeeping forms have traditionally been available in office supply stores, but since personal computers have become so popular, these types of forms have become scarce. This is because hundreds of computer programs of every kind have been produced for desktop computers, including accounting programs. Computerized accounting is discussed later in this chapter. These programs work very well, but there is still a need for manual pen and ink bookkeeping in many cases. It turns out that if these forms were available they would be very expensive. The three journals, the ledger, and their post binders would cost between $120 and $150. Fortunately there are worthy substitutes. They are accountant's analysis pads, and they can be purchased in all office supply stores. They are available in a variety of columnar formats, and they come drilled for three-ring binders. The total amount spent for these books would be a fraction of the cost of the accounting forms, between $20 and $30.

There are three levels of systems that can be employed in church accounting. They range from manual pen and ink systems to pegboard systems to computer accounting programs. Each of these will be explained in detail, along with specific instructions on how to install and operate them. We will start with pen and ink systems and then discuss pegboards and computerized accounting.

31

Cash Receipts Journal

This is the first of three journals in a pen and ink system. It has several columns and the first step in setting it up is to place headings at the tops of the columns. The first column is used to record the dates of the transactions. The second column is headed Cash and all cash receipts are entered in it. The number of other columns depends on how many types of revenue the church has. There must be a column for each type of revenue, such as Tithes and Offerings, Sunday school, Missions, Youth Group, and other categories of revenues. In selecting the form for the cash receipts journal, be sure that it has enough columns to accommodate the several types of revenues the church has.

Samples can be viewed at any office supply store.

The date of the deposit slip should be entered in the Date column, and the amount is entered in the Cash column. Then the sources of the cash received are entered in the respective revenue columns. The cash count tickets, discussed in chapter 2, contain the required information for these columns. The next to the last column in this journal should be labeled Other, and there should be space to the right to explain where the money came from. Occasionally an amount is received which is not a revenue. Such a receipt is entered in the Other column along with an explanation. A good example is a bank loan. The amount of the loan is deposited and recorded in the Cash column. It is also recorded in the Other column accompanied with words of explanation, such as Note Payable. Recording the types of revenue and other cash receipts in this way makes it possible to provide complete information for the monthly and annual financial reports.

Cash Payments Journal

This is the second journal that we need. Since there are more expenses than revenues, this journal will need several more columns than the cash receipts journal. An analysis pad with twelve or thirteen columns is recommended. There is a date column, a wide column in which to write the payee of the check, and a column for the check number. The checks are pre-numbered and all check numbers must be accounted for, including voided checks.

That is why, when you void a check, you should enter it in the cash payments journal and mark it VOID. The first amount column should be headed Cash, followed by expense account titles such as Utilities, Supplies, Bus Expenses, Salaries and Wages along with the related payroll deductions, and any other expenses associated with church operations. Mortgage payments should be divided between interest and principal, and columns must be headed Mortgage Payable for the principle portion of the payment and Interest Expense for the interest portion. The next to the last column should be titled Other, because occasionally there are expenditures which cannot be classified in one of the existing columns. There should be space to the right in which to write words explaining the expenditure. As with the cash receipts journal, accounting for expenses in this way will make monthly and annual financial reporting easy and informative.

General Journal

The purpose of this journal is to record transactions which do not involve cash inflow or outflow. Most of these occur at year end and take the form of adjusting entries, such as depreciation, and closing entries. An occasional general journal entry could occur during the year, but there will not be many.

The general journal has a date column, a wide explanation column for account titles, and two amount columns. Therefore, a two-column analysis pad is what is needed.

Pegboard Systems

These are the high-tech versions of pen and ink accounting. Actually, they are not that high tech, but they do represent a form of automation and they provide increased efficiency. They consist of a folding board with a stainless steel writing surface with short steel pegs along the left side on which to station specially designed forms. They are also called "one-write systems." We can illustrate why by using payroll accounting as an example.

Payroll is a very repetitive process which requires three documents containing essentially the same information. They are a payroll check, a payroll journal, and an individual earnings record for

33

each employee. Each contains the employee's name, social security number, hours worked, gross pay, payroll tax deductions, and other deductions such as group insurance and pension plan contributions. With a completely manual system, the payroll check is prepared containing all of that information. It is then copied onto the payroll journal, and copied again onto the individual earnings record.

There are two problems here. One is the waste of time in writing the same information three times. The other is the boredom inherent in repetitive work. In an organization with as many as a dozen employees, the mind is apt to wander during all of this copying, and this increases the probability of error. We all know that in payroll accounting there is no margin for error; complete 100 percent accuracy is the norm. Anything less is unacceptable. What is the answer to this dilemma? A pegboard system is an excellent solution.

The payroll journal forms have a series of holes which are positioned on the pegs on the left side of the pegboard. Individual earnings records are printed on NCR (No Carbon Required) paper and are placed over the payroll journal one at a time as each employee's check is written. The payroll checks have carbon strips on the back, and they are also placed on the pegs. The pegboard allows all three documents to be perfectly aligned so that when the check is written the information is transferred to the individual earnings record through the carbon strips, and in turn is transferred to the payroll journal through the NCR paper. Therefore, when the check is written the other two documents are written at the same time. Consequently, productivity is greatly increased and there are no copy mistakes.

There are pegboard systems for every accounting activity, including cash receipts. However, one-write cash receipt packages are not very useful for most organizations. They are used primarily by veterinarians, dentists, and other health professionals.

There are several excellent vendors of pegboard systems such as McBee Systems and Safeguard Business Systems. They are all good, but Safeguard distributors provide outstanding service. McBee and Safeguard can be found in the Yellow Pages under Business Forms and Systems.

The most versatile and inexpensive package for churches is a starter set for a combined cash payments and payroll system. It consists of the pegboard, a package of journals, a supply of individual earnings records, a stack of printed checks, and a box of window envelopes. For Safeguard customers, the distributor will set up the system and provide training for the user as part of the cost.

A pegboard system is not a required part of the accounting system, but it is a streamlined way to handle the cash payments function.

The Ledger

Journals are often referred to as books of original entry because all transactions are entered in them first. The ledger is referred to as the book of final entry, because all entries in the ledger are transferred from the journals. The ledger is made up of accounts. Visualize a ring binder with many pages. Each page contains an account, and the account titles correspond to those at the top of the journal columns. Every organization has many accounts and they are all located in the ledger, one account per page. At the end of the month, the journal columns are added and the totals are transferred to the ledger accounts. The term for this transfer process is posting.

There are five classifications of accounts. They are assets, liabilities, equity, revenues, and expenses. Let's become familiar with each one.

Assets are what the organization owns. Cash, petty cash, savings accounts, building fund, land, buildings, furnishings, equipment, vans, and buses are typical asset accounts of churches.

Liabilities are what the organization owes — its debts. Notes payable, mortgages payable, and the deductions from payroll are typical liabilities of any church.

Equity represents the ownership interest. A church is a corporation owned by its members and governed by its board. The amount of a church's equity is the difference between its assets and liabilities. Liabilities represent the creditors' claims on the assets and equity represents the members' share. In a church that is completely debt free, there is no ownership interest other than that of the members. In this case, equity is equal to the assets. The name of the equity account is Net Assets. This is a very descriptive term, because the definition of net assets is total assets minus total liabilities.

Revenues represent the income earning activities of the organization. In a merchandising company they are sales, in a law firm they are fees, and in a real estate agency they are commissions. The titles of a church's revenue accounts are tithes and offerings, missions, Sunday school, building fund, and all other types of cash receipts related to the church's operations. A bank loan does not produce revenue, however; it is a liability.

Expenses are the operating costs of the organization. For a church they include utilities, salaries and wages, maintenance, the church's portion of Social Security and fringe benefits, interest, and all other normal costs of operation.

These are the five classifications of accounts, and they are present in the accounting systems of all organizations. Obviously, every organization does not use the same accounts because each designs its own chart of accounts to meet its needs. Thus we can safely say that no two organizations will have the same account structure. Therefore, a church will organize its accounts and its ledger in a way that fulfills its unique operational requirements.

Ledger account forms have a date column, a wide explanation column that is not used, and three amount columns labeled Debit, Credit, and Balance. The Cash account should be the first account in the ledger.

A Very Useful Tool

You may have noticed that we have not yet used the terms debit and credit. It is certainly possible to do accounting without knowing about debits and credits, and this is frequently the case. However, they make accounting work much easier. Understandably, some people hesitate to enter unknown territory, and these terms are not household words. The good news is that they are simple to learn, and once learned they make life easy for those involved in accounting. Remember that accounting is taught in high school, and high school sophomores have no difficulty in understanding debits and credits. These rules are so easy that one can learn them over the lunch hour and still have time for lunch.

Below is a diagram that illustrates the complete rules of debits and credits. Notice that they involve the five classifications of accounts. Take a few minutes and learn these rules. You should know them as well as your own name or Social Security number. When someone asks for your Social Security number you don't say, "Let me think about it," you just reel it off. Likewise, if someone asks you what kind of a balance Notes Payable should have, you should just say "credit."

DEBITS	CREDITS
• **Increase assets**	• **Decrease assets**
• **Decrease liabilities and equity**	• **Increase liabilities and equity**
• **Decrease revenues**	• **Increase revenues**
• **Increase expenses**	• **Decrease expenses**

The normal balance of an account is what is required to increase it.

Let's see if we can apply these concepts. You will recall that in the section on the cash receipts journal the amount of incoming cash is recorded in the cash column and the sources of the cash inflow are recorded in the revenue columns. Also, in the section on the cash payments journal, the amount of the check is recorded in the cash column and what the money was spent for is recorded in the expense columns. In both cases, the amount of the transaction is recorded twice. This is the nature of double entry accounting. All transactions have two parts, and both parts are recorded. When transactions are recorded, the result is increases and decreases in various accounts. In our accounting systems we could use the terms increase and decrease, or plus and minus, and the system would work. Believe it or not, though, these terms are clumsy and difficult to use. We have found through five centuries of successful use that the terms debit and credit are very efficient and economical in time and space.

Since every transaction has two parts, one part is a debit and the other part is a credit. Therefore, in analyzing transactions, the relevant questions are, "What account do I debit?" and "What account do I credit?" You answer these questions by applying the debit and credit rules shown above. As an illustration, let's go back to our cash receipts journal. The Wednesday evening offering is taken and the bank deposit is made the next day. In entering the transaction, the treasurer must determine what accounts to debit and credit. Follow this reasoning: Cash is an asset and it is being increased. According to the rules, the cash account is debited. Where did the cash come from? According to the cash count ticket it is tithes and offerings. Tithes and offerings are revenues and they are being increased. The rules say that revenues are increased by credits. Therefore the tithes and offerings account is credited.

We can conclude, then, that the cash column in the cash receipts journal is a debit column and the revenue columns are credit columns.

To continue the illustration, let's consider the cash payments journal. The mail brings an invoice for church supplies and Sunday school literature. After determining that the purchase was authorized, the treasurer writes a check on the date the invoice is due to be paid. In entering the check, the treasurer reasons that a check decreases cash, cash is an asset, and the rules call for a credit to cash. The two other accounts are expenses, and they are being increased. The rules say that increases in expenses require debits. Therefore, the entry is a credit to cash and debits to the two expense accounts. Note that this entry contains two debits and one credit, and the two debits are equal in amount to the credit.

We can conclude, then, that in the cash payments journal the cash column is a credit column and the expense columns are debit columns. Cash payments journals often have columns for payroll deductions next to the salaries and wages column. Payroll deductions are liabilities. Therefore, according to the rules, these are credit columns.

It is a good idea to label the columns of the cash receipts and cash payments journals by writing Debit or Credit below the account titles.

A major benefit of using debits and credits is that in every transaction debits and credits must be equal. This assures that the books are in balance at all times. The books sometimes get out of balance, and this is always caused by the inequality of debits and credits. The genius of the debit and credit procedure is that it provides automatic detection of errors. A ledger that does not balance proves that mistakes have been made in the accounting process. These errors are then investigated, discovered, and corrected. A ledger that balances may contain errors, but these are due to other causes. Because they place a high priority on correctness and accuracy, accountants have devised ways to locate and correct these other types of errors. The balancing feature inherent in double entry accounting, with its debits and credits, makes a formidable contribution to the reliability of records, which is part of internal control.

The double entry system is universal among companies. All organizations design their systems according to their own needs, and they all enter transactions in journals with debits and credits, post the monthly totals to ledgers in the form of debits and credits, and check to see that their books remain in balance. Although all organizations design their systems specifically for their own use, they all have the same common characteristics.

Accounting Programs For The Computer

As in a good meal, we have saved the best for last. There is nothing wrong with a pen and ink system; it gets the job done. When a pegboard system is used for cash payments, the job is done even better. Nevertheless, no pen and ink system can come close to a personal computer equipped with a good accounting program.

I have tested about a dozen accounting programs which were specifically designed for desktop computers. My purpose was to identify the best accounting program that I could recommend to clients. I tested these programs by using the practice set assigned to my beginning accounting students as a course requirement. This was very practical because I already had the solution. I could determine the value of the accounting program by comparing its results with the practice set's solution.

The programs tested ranged from useless to outstanding. I found several that were quite good, but one of them had to be better than all the others. By further testing I was able to identify the best one of the group. It is QuickBooks, a product of Intuit, Inc. There are three levels of QuickBooks: Basic, Pro, and Premier. QuickBooks Basic will serve our purpose quite satisfactorily. As of this writing its cost is about $180. It is available at computer and office supply stores, or you may order directly from Intuit by calling toll free at 1-888-729-1996, 1-800-433-8810, or online at www.quickbooks.com.

QuickBooks' advertising states that you do not have to know anything about accounting or be familiar with debits and credits in order to use it. This is true. Now that you know something about debits and credits you are better prepared than some users of QuickBooks.

Of course, the first requirement for using QuickBooks is to have a computer. Many churches already have one and it probably will work if it has a recent version of Microsoft Windows. If the church's computer and operating system are not quite up-to-date, this is an excellent opportunity to acquire a replacement. Similarly, if the church does not yet have a computer, now is the time to get one. It appears that desktop computers are becoming more powerful and less expensive over time. There are many excellent computer stores as well as large electronic and appliance retailers which sell computer equipment. Two computer companies, Dell and Gateway, sell directly to customers, while other fine computers, such as Compaq and Hewlett-Packard, are sold in retail stores. The selected computer should be one of the well-known brands because they have earned their reputations with high quality products and good customer service. Unfamiliar brands should be avoided.

Many computers come bundled with some truly outstanding software. There are different versions of Microsoft Office, a suite containing several excellent programs. Microsoft Office-Standard contains the four basic programs needed for a complete system: Word for word processing, Excel for spreadsheet number crunching, PowerPoint for graphics presentations, and Outlook for e-mail. Widely held opinion is that Word is the best word processor and Excel is the best electronic spreadsheet. Therefore, when faced with a choice of several good computers, choose the one that is equipped with Microsoft Office-Standard, if possible. Another software package that is a worthy substitute is Microsoft Works. It has all the programs you need and more, but it does not contain PowerPoint.

You will need a printer, and the good news is that fine printers are quite inexpensive. There are several name brand ink jet color printers on the market for very low prices. Epson, Lexmark, Canon, and Hewlett-Packard printers are some of the highly regarded printers that are available at low cost. Ink jet printers are almost as good as laser printers, and they are much less expensive.

The Blessings Of QuickBooks

This accounting system performs the same functions as a pen and ink system. It records the usual cash receipts, cash payments, and general journal entries, but it records them easier and better. An example is that posting to the ledger is automatic. It has a good manual and instructions to introduce beginners to the program.

After installing the program, the first step is to set up your organization. There are 23 different types of businesses from which to choose, including Other. There is not one for Church, but there is one for Nonprofit Organization. This one should work, but if not, choose Other. When you choose a type of business, you automatically get a preset chart of accounts. You may use this chart of accounts or design your own. It is usually beneficial to use the chart of accounts provided, add any needed accounts, and ignore the accounts you don't need. These options will allow you to obtain the chart of accounts that reflects the church's operations.

As we learned in pen and ink accounting, almost all transactions are cash receipts and cash payments. When you record a bank deposit, QuickBooks places the amount in the cash account, and it asks you for the account numbers or account titles of the revenue accounts. It automatically enters the deposit in the check register and debits cash and credits the revenue accounts in the ledger. A few key strokes and clicks of the mouse are all you need.

When an organization begins using QuickBooks it already has a supply of checks. It should continue using those checks until they run out. When you write a check and prepare to enter it, a picture of a check appears on the monitor. Type in the date, check number, payee, amount, address (if needed), and memo. Quick-Books removes the amount from the cash account, and it asks you for the account numbers or account titles of the expense accounts. It automatically credits cash and debits the expense accounts in the ledger.

A couple of months before your supply of checks is used up, order replacements from QuickBooks. A catalog and order blank are included with the manual. There are three styles of checks available: standard, wallet, and voucher. Voucher checks are the most useful because they are useful for payroll as well as for paying other bills. They come in single sheets and with one or two copies. Single sheet checks are quite satisfactory. There are three designs from which to choose: classic, prestige, and antique. They are all the same price. Also order a box of window envelopes. They have two windows, the upper one for the return address and the lower one for the payee's name and address. QuickBooks' checks make life easy because you can write the checks on the computer, print them, and mail them in the special envelopes. Entry in the check register is automatic.

Recurring checks, those for payments which are written each month, can be placed in memory. A couple of clicks of the mouse is all that is needed to write the checks. They can also be scheduled for a certain day of the month, and they are written automatically when the computer is turned on that day.

At the end of the month, when the bank statement is received, you can do the bank reconciliation with QuickBooks.

QuickBooks also does payroll accounting. It will write the payroll checks, bring the employee earnings records up to date, as well as record the net pay, payroll deductions, and compensation expense in the ledger. At the end of each quarter, it will prepare the Employer's Quarterly Federal Tax Return, Form 941, Schedule B

(Form 941), and the Employer's Annual Federal Unemployment Tax Return, Form 940. At the end of the year it will print the Wage and Tax Statements, Forms W-2 and the summary, Form W-3.

End Of Period Reporting

After the last transaction of the month is entered, financial reports can be printed immediately. At the end of the year, when all the transactions have been entered and adjusting entries have been made in the general journal, annual financial statements can be printed. Preparing timely financial reports has always been a chronic problem for church treasurers and secretaries. With QuickBooks this is no longer a problem. Click on a report, type the proper dates, and the report appears on the monitor. It can then be edited, corrected, and printed. QuickBooks is known for its ease in bookkeeping and reporting.

A Specialized Accounting System

QuickBooks is a versatile, high quality, inexpensive general purpose program that can be used for many types of organizations, including churches. However, to complete our discussion of computerized accounting systems, we should recognize that there are some excellent systems specifically designed for church accounting. Shelby Systems is one of those.

A list of what a Shelby System can do is quite impressive. Its most basic package, the Bronze Collection, will handle general ledger, check writing, bank reconciliation, contributions, membership, and Pose 'n' Print. The last item is truly fascinating. It stores individual pictures as well as family photos. Pastors can look at a member's picture while speaking on the telephone, and pictures can be printed on individual information sheets. Further, this module can be used to print the church's pictorial directory.

The Silver Collection adds attendance and prospects modules. The Gold Collection adds accounts payable and payroll. The Platinum Collection adds purchase order, fixed assets, accounts receivable, miscellaneous names and addresses, registrations, and check-in modules. It appears that this collection would be necessary for only the largest churches. It seems that the Bronze Collection plus the payroll module would be sufficient for most medium-sized churches.

There is no question that Shelby Systems provide outstanding accounting and other related church programs. However, their cost would represent a major financial investment for a small or medium-sized church. As of this writing the cost of the Bronze Collection is $1,995, and the payroll module would be in addition to that. Annual support is $490 after the first six months. Nevertheless, for a church that needs this level of service, this would be a reasonable investment.

Information about the company is as follows:
Shelby Systems
51 Germantown Court, Suite 300
Cordova, TN 38018
1-800-877-0222
www.shelbyinc.com

Should The Church Have An Audit?

"The CPAs are auditing the books" is a common complaint despite the fact that it is actually untrue. Auditing is a widely misunderstood procedure, so let's clear up the confusion.

Certified public accountants provide three levels accounting service to clients. They are audit, review, and compilation, and all three are frequently referred to as "auditing" by the general public.

Auditing is the highest level of accounting service as well as the most time consuming and expensive. Actually, an audit is an examination of the financial statements, not the books, although they examine the books, transaction documents, contracts, minutes of the board of directors, and everything else in the course of the audit. Auditors obtain evidentiary matter, both internal and external, and external evidence is considered the more reliable. In gathering external evidence they confirm bank accounts and notes directly with the banks, confirm accounts receivable balances directly with the customers, and observe the counting of the physical inventory. The end result is an audit report which expresses an opinion on the quality of the financial statements. The Securities and Exchange Commission (SEC) requires all corporations whose stock is traded in the financial markets to have audits. Consequently, there are few voluntary audits, although there are some.

The second level, review, is a high quality service in which the CPAs do not obtain external evidence, and it is much less expensive. It is an examination of internal evidence and analytical review. This procedure provides considerable assurance of the appropriateness of the financial statements, although it is not as good as an audit. Nevertheless, it is acceptable for most purposes other than reporting to the SEC. The end result is a review report which states that nothing has come to the CPAs' attention that the financial statements are not appropriate.

The lowest level of accounting service is compilation. In such an engagement, the CPAs take the client's books and prepare financial statements from them. They do little, if any, examination of evidence or other analytical work. It is, of course, the least expensive of the three services. The compilation report says that the statements have not been audited or reviewed and the accountant does not express an opinion or any other form of assurance on them. Since a compilation provides almost no oversight of the financial system and those who operate it, I do not recommend it. The major benefit of engaging a CPA is the advice and guidance of an independent, outside observer. This is present in an audit and a review, but not in a compilation. In my opinion, a compilation is of little value.

Now let's go back to the original question, "Should the church have an audit?" Probably not. Some nonprofit organizations have audits because their boards desire them. For this reason a church could have an audit if the board so desires. However, for most entities other than publicly traded companies, a review is sufficient. It provides outside oversight, a look at internal control, professionally prepared financial statements, and a meaningful accountant's report to accompany them. Accordingly, I always recommend a review.

A Short Summary

We have come a long way from the beginning of this chapter. It appears that the best of all worlds is available to us. We learned about internal control in chapter 2, and in this chapter we learned the basics of accounting. We also introduced two excellent computerized accounting systems, and we discussed how to use a CPA firm to the best advantage for a reasonable cost. This can be one of the building blocks for outstanding church administration.

McBee, Safeguard, Intuit, QuickBooks, Dell, Gateway, Compaq, Hewlett-Packard, Microsoft Office, Microsoft Word, Microsoft Excel, Microsoft PowerPoint, Microsoft Outlook, Microsoft Works, Epson, Lexmark, Canon, and Shelby Systems are trademarks or registered trademarks of their respective companies and are hereby acknowledged.

Chapter 5

Financial Management, The Road To Success

I once attended a large Christian Church (Disciples of Christ) in a medium-sized Indiana city. Similar to most mainline churches with a long history, it was originally located in the central section of the city close to the business district. Like many such churches it outgrew the building and found it necessary to relocate. It purchased an industrialist's mansion in a quiet, residential neighborhood in a beautiful, park-like setting the size of a city block. By the time services began in the new location the property was paid for. The church eventually constructed a large beautiful building on the grounds, and the mansion was then used for offices, meetings, parties, and Sunday school classes. The new building was paid for by the time it was completed. In recent years the church built a major addition to the building that was so well designed that it seemed to be a part of the original structure. It was completely paid for on the day it was dedicated. This church has never paid a cent of interest. It would be difficult to find a better example of successful church financing.

Less successful examples are very easy to find. We all know of churches in buildings they cannot afford and which have a difficult time making the mortgage payments. Such churches are usually high on hope and low on accomplishment.

This low success level affects every aspect of ministry. When mortgage payments are difficult to pay all other obligations are difficult to pay, also. Required expenses, such as salaries and utilities, become problems. Elective expenses, such as missions and evangelism, are usually overlooked or postponed. This puts the treasurer in a very uncomfortable position, and it doesn't improve the pastor's peace of mind, either.

It would be logical for churches to try to follow the Indiana church's example as closely as possible and avoid those at the other extreme.

Financing Objectives

In business, finance is concerned with two major activities, providing the funds required by the organization when needed and the efficient investment of excess funds. The latter activity is rarely a concern of churches because the normal condition is a shortage of funds rather than an excess of them. If churches should have more cash than they need for current operations, they usually prefer to pay off debt, which is good financial management, or to invest in missions, evangelism, and other important ministries, which are also good investments. Therefore, the major thrust of effective financial management is to identify financial goals and obtain the funds to meet them. All churches have two primary financial problems, cash flow for ongoing operations and financing the physical plant. These two problems exist in churches of all sizes, but they are particularly acute in growing churches. Such churches periodically need more space, more space requires construction, and construction requires finances. These two problems are distinctly separate; funds needed for operating expenses cannot be used for construction, and building funds are not available for ongoing expenses.

It would be a wonderful idea to follow the example of the church that paid for everything in advance. This avoids debt and, of course, mortgage payments. However, good financial management also includes the proper use of debt. All business corporations have debt on their balance sheets because it enables them to accomplish well-defined objectives with optimal timing. Those objectives could be accomplished without debt, but by incurring indebtedness they can be achieved according to an established timetable. This is also true for a church. By financing the building program, the congregation can get into the building much earlier. It follows, then, that the church can begin accomplishing the Great Commission earlier. Actually, there is nothing wrong with correctly administered debt.

For a church to move into a building that is totally paid for contributes to a very comfortable existence. No payments, no interest, and no second offerings on Sunday mornings. The key to going into debt is to maintain that comfort level and the payments at the same time. Comfort and payments can coexist, and this is where financial management comes in. The answer is to take on only the amount of debt that can be met easily and to make sure that the funds are always available when the payments become due. To do otherwise can be disastrous.

Fortunately, this is easier to accomplish than you might think. Consider the church that pays for everything in advance. In order to do this it had to engage in some serious advance fund raising. To a lesser extent, similar advance fund raising is necessary for the church which finances its building with a mortgage loan. How much should the church have in reserve for mortgage payments? There is no standard answer to this question, but financial advisors have suggested to individual clients that they should have about six months income in reserve to meet unforeseen cash demands. This is also good advice for churches. Prior to signing a mortgage note, the church should raise an amount sufficient to cover six months of payments, and this amount should be invested in a certificate of deposit or other interest bearing account. With such an amount in reserve, the church can overcome financial difficulties as they arise, such as an economic downturn, a needed overhaul of the church bus, a new compressor for the air conditioning system, or anything else that might occur.

Obviously, every building program is preceded by a fund drive. Money is needed to purchase land, make the down payment, and provide other advance cash requirements. The initial building fund should be structured to include the six months' reserve account. Fortunately, congregations usually rally to a good cause, and a building program causes much excitement and support among the congregation. With such support, meeting the building fund goal should not be an insurmountable problem.

What if something unforeseen does not occur? The good news is that financial success breeds financial success. With a comfortable cash balance, month to month financial pressure is removed from the pastor to the point that he can expend his energy on the really important parts of his ministry. It is not uncommon for well-managed churches to make double mortgage payments and to have a mortgage burning ceremony several years ahead of schedule. Another advantage of good financial management is that congregations become aware of good stewardship when implemented by the pastor and the board. Church attendance often declines in the presence of financial pressure, but increases when the congregation has evidence of financial success. Making double payments on the mortgage sends a very positive message. As they say, nothing succeeds like success.

Bible schools and seminaries do not provide a great amount of training in business administration, and in this respect many pastors are not well equipped for handling the business side of church operations. The good news is that such training is not necessary. The major ingredient of good financial management is common sense, and pastors usually have plenty of that. Any pastor with initiative and an innovative mind can solve a growing church's financial problems. Pastors are not required to solve them alone; they can utilize the services of people in their congregations who are skilled in these matters. Such professional people are often on church boards, and they certainly should be on the building and finance committees.

It is widely understood in Christian circles that the Lord deserves the best that we have to offer. This, of course, includes the same sound financial principles that businesses follow. A church that is well managed financially is a blessing to the community and a fitting testimony of God's providence for all to see.

Whither Budgeting?

Eventually, the church building is completed and occupied, and the financial emphasis shifts to making the payments and meeting the expenses. Should the church have a budget?

Many things can be said about budgeting. It is difficult, boring, time consuming, and inaccurate. It is also necessary for financial success.

Successful businesses use budgets. To be sure, there are some profitable companies that do not budget, and there are some failed companies that do, but there is a high correlation between business success and budgeting. As part of the process, businesses do what is called "profit planning." They actually plan to make profits. For many businesses, if profits were not planned there would not be any. A profit is not the result of a happy accident; it is actually built into the budgeting process. Can this be true of churches? Certainly. Although churches are nonprofit organizations, they still must have revenues greater than expenses, and that is the definition of profit in business enterprises. Although budgeting may be difficult and boring, it is not extremely difficult but it probably is extremely boring. Considering the benefits, we should do it anyway. Fortunately, there is a learning curve associated with budgeting; it gets easier as time goes on.

For an established church, next year's budget starts with this year's financial statement, the one that reports revenues and expenses. The budgeted financial statement is composed of this year's amounts updated with current information and growth projections. Each revenue item will either increase or decrease. Based on current knowledge and an estimate of growth, you can reflect these increases and decreases in budgeted revenues. Likewise, each expense item can be expected to go up or down in the coming year. You can depict those changes based on current information and anticipated growth. Just start at the top of the financial statement and arrive at a budgeted figure for every line item. When you get to the bottom of the page the budget is finished.

Remember that the budget is not a prediction but an estimate. That is why it is inaccurate; estimates are always imprecise. A budget is not required to be correct; it is only required to be a guide to the future. It contains expectations and goals, not prophecy. As in a business, it is a financial plan. Without it, guidance is nonexistent. With a budget, the pastor and board can exercise control over future events. Without one, events are in control. It is much better when church management is in charge of events, and budgeting makes this possible. Remember that a budget is not a straitjacket for restricting spending. It is a guide for the future and a roadmap for the present. Financial statements are historical in nature and backward looking. Budgets point to the future and are forward looking.

51

There are two characteristics of budgeted expenses. Some expenses are required in the operation while some are discretionary. For example, in a business utilities are required expenses while advertising is discretionary. In a church, many expenses are mandatory, such as supplies and salaries, while others are optional, such as a musical program or a holiday dinner party. A budget facilitates the planning of these important events, helps determine priorities, and indicates funding needs.

There are two concepts for funding discretionary expenditures, and these are common, if not unique, to churches. One is for each program to be self-supporting and responsible for its own funding. The other is to finance special events from the general fund.

As an example, let's consider organizing a youth softball team. There is some cost involved and it can be estimated. One way of funding the program is to forecast how many will be involved, divide the estimated cost by that number, compute the amount per person, and charge each participant that amount. In this way the program cost is covered without using funds committed for other purposes. On the other hand, the team could be financed from the general fund under the assumption that the purpose of that fund is to enable important ministries such as this to be carried on. Both concepts are valid and are regularly employed in churches.

A great author of management textbooks wrote of the concept of "unflinching control." With a well thought out budgetary plan, the pastor, the board, and the Holy Spirit can come close to achieving that level of control in church management.

Conclusion

A basic tenet of economics is that more is better than less. A related concept is that success is better than failure. This is true in all levels of society, including churches. We have already established that the Lord's work deserves the best we have to offer. In the dichotomy of success and failure, excellent financial management helps accomplish the one and avoid the other.

Chapter 6

Management, The Art Of The Possible

A large part of management is simply common sense. By using common sense and goodwill in dealing with others, anyone can become an excellent manager.

Managing People

Before I started my professional career I began to formulate some management theories which I would use in the future when I would be a manager. These theories went something like this. If you want people to do something, it is better to ask them to do it rather than tell them to do it. When it is done, show your appreciation and thank them for it. It is true that they are paid for doing their jobs, but thank them anyway. If a task is done well, tell them about it, and telling them in public is very acceptable. Conversely, if a task is not done well, you have to tell them about that, also. This must be done in a kind and tactful manner and always in private, never in public. The purpose is to help the employees correct their mistakes and do better the next time. The goal is to encourage people to improve their performance, to help them do their very best, and these principles always work. These are tenets of good business. Did these theories work for me? They worked beautifully and I became a very successful manager in two different companies. Will they work in church? Of course they will.

A pastor of a church wears two hats. He is the spiritual leader, but he is also the president of a corporation. It has been said that every business is a people business, and dealing with the people of an organization is one of the most important duties of management. This is true for all organizations and it is certainly true for a church. Most churches, including some small ones, have a staff of one or more associate pastors with definite and distinct responsibilities. There is usually an office staff consisting of at least one secretary. In addition, there is a large group of volunteers without whom many church programs would not be possible. All of these people have a common goal, to serve God in the stated mission of the church, but to achieve it they need direction. Of course, the ultimate responsibility is the pastor's. This makes it obvious that management skills are needed for successful pastoral leadership.

A good manager is polite and courteous, and these characteristics encourage good performance, high productivity, and outstanding loyalty. These are the end results of effective management. Bad manners and discourtesy are not acceptable and must never be allowed to enter the working environment. There are no occasions in which harsh language is beneficial. Politeness, concern for others, and following the precepts of the Bible, particularly chapter 13 of 1 Corinthians, are what one needs to be an excellent manager of human resources. Learning management skills is not difficult; it is actually an easy challenge in a continuing process. Employment of these methods will ensure success in effective and efficient church administration.

There is a major mistake that some churches make, particularly some of the evangelical churches. It is a practice of these churches that, when the pastor resigns, the associates are expected or required to resign also. The reason given for this is that the new pastor, after he arrives, will be able to select his own staff. Also, the new pastor might feel threatened by the existing associates. The supposition is that the congregation will be loyal to the associates rather than to the new pastor. This practice has destroyed the careers of many young ministers, and it has brought permanent damage to many churches. It is difficult to imagine a business corporation behaving in this way. When the president resigns should all of the vice presidents resign, also? Such a move would leave the company without any leadership. The vice presidents need to remain in place, discharging their responsibilities as usual, because they are necessary to maintain the continuity of the operation. This is no less true of a church. With the departure of the pastor the associates become even more important, and they often accept additional responsibilities because continuity of leadership must be maintained. The best advice is to leave the pastoral staff intact to guide the church during the transition period and to provide the professional support needed by the incoming pastor. A well-trained staff already working together is a valuable asset to any new pastor, as well as the church. If an incoming pastor has trouble with this, he should strive to become knowledgeable of the existing situation and count his blessings.

What about the perceived threat against the pastor on the part of the associates and the perceived disloyalty of the congregation? Fortunately, these problems are more imagined than real. A pastor with the call of God on his life has no reason to feel threatened by anyone, especially associates, and new pastors do not have any difficulty in gaining the love and respect of their congregations in a relatively short time.

Managing The Office

In addition to managing human resources, let's direct our attention to the other problem of church administration, office management. Office management is not an isolated topic; it dovetails with accounting and internal control. These are integral parts of running any office, and chapters 2 and 4 covered these topics in detail. Now let's deal with what's left.

The beauty of management is that, to quote a cliché, the whole is greater than the sum of its parts. The buzz word is "synergism." When those with administrative responsibility work as a team, much more can be accomplished than if those same individuals work alone. Therefore, the team approach is highly productive.

For the team approach to work, the top manager has to set the tone. He must establish a good example for others to follow. For example, the ideal manager doesn't only get to work on time; he gets there early. He is not a clock watcher; he does not display a strong desire to leave the moment that closing time arrives.

Here is an illustrative example. Early in my career, I was accounting supervisor in a wonderful new scientific company in Santa Monica. I was on the same organizational level as the purchasing agent. One day my car was in the shop for repairs, and I had to leave right at closing time to pick it up. That was the first time I ever saw the front door at that particular time of day, and I was almost run over by the purchasing agent and others trying to get out the door as quickly as possible. I survived in this company; he did not. This is not to say that starting early and staying late is a guarantee of longevity on the job, but it is indicative of a mental attitude that shows dedication to one's job. I can think of no vocation in which this is not an important ingredient for success. The moral of the story is this: To be an effective leader, the manager must set a good example for others to follow. You may be assured that they will follow it.

Nuts And Bolts

A major part of efficient office management is a good filing system. Such a system is easier to devise than you might think. So is a poor one. I was a member of Masterworks Chorale, a classical singing group, for several years. I was elected to the board of directors and eventually became president. They already had an accounting system, which I improved, and an intricate filing system. It was so intricate that it required an index to locate any file. The rule was that when someone used the index it should be replaced immediately in its designated location. One day someone did not put it back where it belonged and the office manager could not find anything. After some angry words, it was eventually located and the filing system was back in business. Obviously, this filing system needed to be redesigned in a way that would enable them to throw out that ridiculous index.

There is a better way. Visualize a new, five-drawer file cabinet. In a business, one group of files is composed of sales invoices. These should be placed in one file drawer and arranged in alphabetical order by customer name. In a church, the counterpart is contribution records, and these should be arranged alphabetically by contributor. What could be simpler? It is true that many churches provide numbered envelopes for the congregation to use for tithes and offerings, but it is still better to file those records in alphabetical order.

Also in a business the next major filing group is vendors. Invoices and the related attached documents, such as requisitions, purchase orders, and receiving reports, should be placed in another drawer and filed alphabetically by vendor. Churches also have vendor invoices and they also should be filed in the same way.

These two drawers can be labeled "Contribution Records" and "Paid Invoices." A third drawer could be labeled "Everything Else." However, that should not be the title printed on the card on the front of the file drawer. An innocuous title such as "General Files" is better. All files other than those pertaining to contributions and purchases can go in there, in alphabetical order, of course. If a significant group of files becomes prominent it will deserve its own section of a file drawer or perhaps an entire drawer.

Always insist on file folders which are letter size, not legal size. One-third cut manila folders are the most useful. Different types of files, hanging folders, are very convenient to use. You might want to check out hanging file kits which are available at office supply stores and most discount stores. One-fifth cut is normal for hanging files. The best way to make file labels, and other labels, is with an inexpensive computer program, Avery DesignPro. It uses Avery labels, of course, and these are probably the best for all purposes, with or without DesignPro.

Incidentally, in buying file cabinets and other office furnishings, you can't do better than Steelcase. You get high quality at good prices. Color is important; gray is depressing and green is passé. The most popular colors are desert sage or desert sand. These colors make a dull office bright and beautiful.

A Good Management Technique

An outstanding managerial policy is to keep the desk clear at all times. Is this even possible? Of course it is, or I wouldn't have brought it up. We have all been in offices where the desk was piled high with all kinds of papers and the walls were lined with files stacked on the floor. Whatever this represents, it is not management. People who do this assure all those who will listen that, don't worry, they are really organized and they can find anything they want. Well, perhaps, but this does not justify such a disorganized and unsightly mess. One should never let the desk and the in-box pile up. It is never necessary and it is counterproductive.

The difference between a clean desk and a messy one is nothing more than a frame of mind. The key is to make the decision in advance to work on everything immediately when it comes to the desk. The opposite is to think, "I'll work on this later," and the paperwork inevitably piles up. The ideal is for the manager to establish the policy, in advance, to solve problems as they arrive rather than at some later time. It is easier than you think, and the result is a well-organized manager working in a well-organized office.

Nevertheless, it is not uncommon for information to come in faster than it can be worked on and for problems to arise faster than they can be solved. We have all experienced this, and it is not always possible to follow the ideal policy of working on everything immediately. How do we handle this? Most desks have a file drawer. It is good to keep a stack of new file folders close by, and when something comes up that cannot be handled immediately, slip it into a folder, write the topic on the tab in pencil, and place it in the desk file drawer. How should they be filed? In alphabetical order, of course, for instant reference. After a while, these files will take up a few inches in the front of the file drawer awaiting action when time becomes available. The desk will remain clear and all of the problems will be solved in due time. It is noteworthy that these principles will work for church pastors and associate pastors as well as corporate presidents and accountants.

Conclusion

This chapter contains the ingredients for pastors of small and medium-sized churches to attain a high level of managerial quality. Although this is not the last word in management theory, any pastor who puts these principles to work can go beyond this chapter, utilize his God-given intelligence, and take whatever additional steps that are needed to lead the church on its path to greatness. There is much more that can be learned about management, but this chapter provides a foundation sufficient to make a significant difference in the church's administration. Many churches are begun without giving any thought to managerial affairs, and any church that follows these concepts is much further ahead than if they were disregarded.

For further enlightenment in this regard, there is an outstanding book by George Barna which can be very helpful for the growing church, *The Habits of Highly Effective Churches*. This book is the result of Dr. Barna's research on how some churches became highly effective. It is available from Barna Research Group's website, www.barna.org. As of this writing the book's cost is from $12 to $13. In addition, when you get into this website you will find many other excellent resources to aid in ministry.

Another fine company that has a multitude of ministry resources is Gospel Light in Ventura, California. Its website is www.gospellight.com.

Avery and DesignPro are registered trademarks of Avery Dennison Corporation.

Chapter 7

Marketing Equals Sharing

Should the church do marketing? Churches have been engaging in marketing since time immemorial; that is, as long as any of us can remember. Advertising in the church page of Saturday newspapers and placing revival posters in shop windows are marketing activities. When we think of marketing, we think of it strictly in a business context, some of which is very respectable, but some is crass and in poor taste. In business, marketing is both honorable and necessary. Can the same be said of churches? Certainly.

What Is Marketing?

Marketing in business is nothing more than meeting the wants and needs of consumers. The great American economic system is remarkable in its capacity to supply the goods and services needed to increase the living standards of a growing population. It not only supplies the goods, it also provides the income for individuals to acquire them. Wants and needs are often confused. The American people have the charming habit of transforming luxuries into necessities. What is a dishwasher, a luxury or a necessity? We all know the answer to that question.

American businesses supply their customers' needs at considerable risk to themselves. They obtain the necessary financing, do the research and development, manufacture the products, and market them in the hope of recovering their costs and making a profit. Marketing enables them to do that, and people are better off because of it. Since people actually need the goods produced by business, marketing can be looked upon as a sharing process by which producers distribute the fruits of their productivity to those who desire them. To determine what consumers want and need and to bring these desired commodities to market require massive commitments of resources, and the end results of those resources are

61

shared with a demanding public. Marketing is the vehicle that makes it possible. The ability of businesses to identify and satisfy the needs of consumers will determine how successful they are.

When we think of marketing, it is common to equate it with advertising. Marketing is more than that, although advertising is an important element of marketing. In fact, advertising is the one aspect of marketing that churches have been doing rather well for a long time. There are many advertising media available, and they all have one characteristic in common, acquaint the community with the church and its ministries. Church advertising in all media should always be attractive and in good taste.

There are a couple of myths associated with advertising and promotion. "Say whatever you want; just spell the name right," and "Even bad news about a product will sell it." These statements have never been true, and that is why advertisers should always insist on high quality in their advertising messages.

A Similarity
A church is not much different from a business in this respect. Churches do not have customers, of course, but they have parishioners who have needs like everyone else. Only the church is in a position to supply those particular needs. God has a vehicle through which to work, and that is the church's unique function. Its success or failure can be traced to its ability to meet the expectations of its consumers. If it does not satisfy their needs, its effectiveness will be limited, and it will fail to follow the Lord's admonition to spread the gospel to those who need God's love and providence.

Examples abound. We have all seen small churches which have been small forever. The reason they remain small is because they simply are not meeting people's needs. We have also seen growing churches which regularly run out of space and require a new building addition every few years. When you see a church with parking problems you can conclude that it is doing something right in providing for the needs of those in the congregation.

The marketing function can be fulfilled by determining what the membership desires and building this information into the church's programs. For example, the weekly services should be designed to appeal to the entire congregation rather than certain segments of it, although the various parts of the congregation should be ministered to individually. Children, youth, married couples, seniors, singles, college students, and others need exciting and inspiring programs directed to their needs, and these programs will inevitably contribute to the growth of the church. Remember, however, that they are parts of the whole, and it is vital that the emphasis be directed toward the entire church body.

Let's consider a case that cries out for a marketing solution. The Sunday evening service has traditionally been very important among evangelical churches. Morning worship usually followed the Sunday school hour and its emphasis was on the spiritual growth and edification of the regular adherents. The evening service has traditionally been an evangelistic outreach, and its emphasis was on spreading the message of Christ to those outside the church and blessing the regular members. This evening service is usually quite exciting with special music, a rousing song from the choir, and a stimulating evangelistic sermon. Visiting quartets, choirs, soloists, and other musical groups may appear in the evening service. In recent years, these services have begun to undergo major changes. They have become less structured. The time may have been changed, and people may have been encouraged to "come as you are." The choir, such as it was, sauntered onto the platform in jeans and T-shirts instead of robes. The music consisted primarily of contemporary songs and choruses. The hymn book was used rarely, if at all. The entire service was conducted in a "hang loose" atmosphere, and evangelistic outreach faded from the agenda. People started to feel that there was not much of importance going on, and attendance began to decline because of lack of interest. Creating interest is what marketing is all about.

This scenario has been repeated in churches all over the country to the point that many have simply discontinued the Sunday evening service, and the churches are worse off because of it. If, before making those changes, the church leaders had given some thought to marketing principles, the Sunday evening service would still be a vital part of the church calendar. It is obvious that no thought was given to what the membership wanted, and even worse, what the membership needed.

On the bright side, some churches, including some newer ones, have revived Sunday evening services with special speakers, traveling singing groups, spirited choir songs, a church quartet, family carry-in dinners, and other imaginative programs. There are many brilliant examples of these programs in several churches across the country in which the Sunday evening service has once again become a dynamic, exciting event.

A Church Coach?

One of the most innovative developments in recent years is the church consultant. An Associated Press article by Rachel Zoll describes how church coaches use marketing to advise congregations about how to attract more parishioners. This article appeared in the *Sacramento Bee* on January 9, 1999. It recounts the success of Dr. and Mrs. Daniel Allen who point out that "Some churches have signs that are unspoken: 'We don't want you here.' " By contrast, churches need signs that say, "We are a warm and loving place." Lainie Allen, who has a master's degree in education, says that churches, like businesses, must reach their target groups. In their consulting assignments they travel the country inspecting everything from the condition of church bathrooms to the peeling paint on the sanctuary walls to the churches' spiritual energy. Signs that say, "Y'all come to our church" do not work. It is ironic that some of the least friendly churches use a rubber stamp with the slogan, "The Friendliest Church in Town."

Polls show that people avoid church for several reasons. They feel pressured to contribute money, they find services boring, and the sermons irrelevant. The Allens note that newcomers decide in the first eleven minutes whether to return. For this reason, cleanliness and the quality of music are very important. Their philosophy is that people need to know that God loves them, and any obstacles to the delivery of this message must be removed.

When Dr. Allen arrives at a church, he immediately takes an inventory. He gets answers to these questions: Is the parking lot paved? Are the bathrooms well marked and clean? Is the church bulletin attractive and informative? Are there designated greeters? Are the sermons relevant? They need to be biblical, of course, but they need to deal with real problems. People often ask the mental question, "So what? How does this help me in my daily life?"

The Allens suggested to one successful pastor that he ask first-time visitors not to contribute when the offering plate comes by. The message is that the church is more interested in their spirit than their money, and this message makes a profound impression on newcomers. You will not be surprised to find that this is a growing church.

This important Associated Press article by Rachel Zoll proves the efficacy of marketing in building a vital and successful church that meets the needs of its members and makes visitors want to become members. The unwritten sign is "God loves you and we want you to be a part of us."

Precaution

A cautionary note is in order. We have already established that a church, in order to grow, must provide what their people want and need. This is not to suggest that a pastor must compromise biblical teachings and sacrifice principle in exchange for popularity. There is never a justification for adulterating the gospel message in order to give people "what they want to hear." In fact, Christians prefer good Bible preaching, and when a pastor delivers it, he is giving them what they need. We must not get the idea that, since marketing is providing what people want, it requires compromising Christian principles. Some of America's oldest and greatest church organizations have suffered serious declines because they have replaced the unadorned Christian message with a social engineering gospel full of political correctness.

George Barna, in his provocative book, *The Frog in the Kettle*, makes eight proposals. Two of them are quite relevant in this context.

1. We must champion Christian morals. If we do not stand up for Christian principles, nobody will.

2. We must refine the thinking of Christians so that they see themselves as ministers of the gospel and as 24-hour marketing agents.

It is difficult to imagine a more eloquent rationale for marketing in the service of God.

Chapter 8

Production Values

When we think of production we usually think of manufacturing. While it is true that manufacturing results in the production of goods, production is not limited to that which is made in factories. In fact, production predates the industrial revolution by a couple of centuries. The plays of Shakespeare are a good example.

The Possibilities Of Production

Can production be associated with the church? After all, production usually refers to material things, objects, properties, and manufacturing. However, consider the Broadway musical, an example of a high level of production that has nothing to do with manufacturing. The producer is one of the most important personages in the musical, and he does not even appear on stage. This is true of plays, motion pictures, stage shows, operas, and television programs. All of these media are productions, and the best ones are said to have high production values.

It does not take much imagination to realize that if an excellent operetta is a good production, an outstanding church service is also a good production. And whether we give it much thought or not, every church service is a production and is produced by someone. Therefore, the only relevant question is this: "Is it a good production or a poor one, and will it have high or low production values?"

Sadly, if production values are not given any thought or effort, low quality church experiences are inevitable. Conversely, high quality church experiences don't just happen, they are caused. The choice is between mediocrity and excellence, and excellence is better. This being the case, it only makes sense to give some serious thought to production, and high production values are a worthy goal for a church.

Actual Experience

Here are two examples which illustrate this point. It has been my pleasure to attend a very large church in a major city. Every minute was filled with inspiring happenings from the opening song to the altar call. There were no wasted moments. Valuable time was not wasted in making announcements because they were already printed in the bulletin. Soloists and singing groups were never introduced. Just before they were scheduled to appear they would gather quietly at the side of the platform, and when their time came they would advance to the platform and perform their songs in a professional manner. Likewise, the choir selection was not announced. At the proper time the director stood, gave the downbeat, and the building was filled with beautiful music. All of these activities were structured in a way that would prepare the congregation for the sermon. When the time came for the sermon, the pastor simply strode to the pulpit and delivered an anointed message that ended with the invitation. When the people left the service, they felt inspired and blessed. It is no surprise that this great church has had space problems for most of its existence. It seems they were always in a building program in order to keep up with the growing congregation. Fortunately, they had a large plot of land that allowed them to expand their facilities when it became necessary.

Here is a contrasting example. A small church in a medium-sized city has had excess seating capacity from its beginning. People entered a poorly lighted sanctuary and the services began with talk. Everyone who did anything talked about it first. The announcements for the coming week required a great deal of talk. It is well known that church bulletins are so economical to prepare that even small churches can afford them, but one gets the impression that spoken announcements provide opportunities for someone to engage in additional talk. Every song was announced and every singer was introduced. A massive amount of time was wasted with incessant talk. By sermon time, there had already been so much talk that the message itself was an anticlimax. The invitation seemed superfluous because the activities preceding it were so uninviting that few people would want to be a part of it. Of course, no thought had

68

been given to the quality of the church services. It is an observable fact that people will not choose to be a part of this type of Christian experience, and that is the reason why there were never any space problems in this church. It goes without saying that this congregation was spared the necessity of raising funds and expanding into bigger and better buildings since they did not have any anticipation of filling the one they had.

Whither Production?

A couple of important questions come to mind:

- Should the church have a producer in charge of producing the church services?
- Since we have established that production values are essential for excellence, who should do the producing?

The answer to the first question is "Definitely not!" We have already established that good production is necessary, but it should always take place in the background, behind the scenes. The terms "production" and "producer" should never be used because of their show business connotations. A close identification of the church with the entertainment industry would make a very bad impression. Technically, an inspiring church service should not be considered a production, but it definitely should contain high production values. It is important to note that production values are not limited to entertainment and church services, but they are present in classroom lectures, business presentations, seminars, conferences, and other public events.

The answer to the second question is, "The pastor." Since he is the spiritual leader, he is responsible for all aspects of the worship services, including the cultivation of production values. It is exciting what an innovative pastor, with the Holy Spirit's guidance, can do to make every worship service a memorable occasion. When production values become an important ingredient of all church services, it is logical to anticipate a growth in attendance because it is natural for people to prefer high quality over low quality in everything. Such a church is a blessing to its congregation and an

69

asset to the community. It is particularly attractive to the unchurched, and it is the church's calling to "bring them in."

I once was involved in some meetings with an outstanding young pastor who began a church in a small southern community. From the beginning it seemed that he couldn't construct buildings fast enough. Eventually the church's Sunday morning attendance exceeded the population of the town. This church not only blessed the people in its own community but also those in the surrounding areas. This pastor was certainly doing something right, and the influence for good that he has had in his general area is immeasurable.

We must be very careful to avoid a show business attitude. In a theatrical production, the producer has a prominent place among the credits. Who should get the credit for a good church service? Without God's presence the pastor, or anyone else, would not be able to organize a Spirit-filled worship service; therefore, God should get the credit because it is his and his alone.

Can We Draw A Conclusion From All This?

We know that marketing is determining what people want and need, and then filling that demand. People always prefer excellence over mediocrity when they spend their money. They also prefer excellence over mediocrity when they spend their valuable time in going to church. Happiness with any product breeds contentment, and contentment breeds growth. High production values are the means for attaining excellence, exceptional quality, contentment, growth, and meeting the Great Commission as commanded in Matthew 28:19. As for production values, the Lord and his people deserve the best we have to offer. Therefore, let's strive to do the best we can for God by insisting on high production values in our church services.

Chapter 9

Putting It All Together

It has always been assumed that the Christian portion of the population was somewhere in the lower part of the socioeconomic totem pole. Christians were considered to be in the bottom half. They were looked upon as somewhat below the level of ordinary folks. Those who held this view were certain that churchgoers were not on the same high plane as they. This has never been true, and it is less true today than ever before.

In sociology, the church is described as a vertical organization, while the American Medical Association, for example, is a horizontal organization. A church has people from all walks of life and every economic level, while the AMA is an association of individuals who are similarly situated, physicians. Members of horizontal organizations, such as the American Institute of Certified Public Accountants and the National Rifle Association, have a commonality of purpose. Although the church population is quite diverse, its members also have a commonality of purpose, which includes the spiritual growth of the congregation, spreading the gospel of Christ, and extending the kingdom of God around the world. That is the beauty of the church; people from all walks of life and all strata of society are welcome to join together to achieve an important shared goal.

Those who hold the erroneous view of Christians do not expect much from them because they presume that Christians, being mediocre people, will produce mediocre results. It often escapes notice, but neither God's people nor their achievements are mediocre. Historically, God has always had adherents at the highest levels of society producing high quality achievements. Although extraordinary quality has not always been attained, ordinary people doing their best for God often produce spectacular results. This is particularly true of those who insist upon excellence and seek his guidance in everything they do.

There is no better example than Johann Sebastian Bach. William F. Buckley, Jr., has correctly described Bach as a gift that God gave to the world, and there is much evidence that this description is accurate. As a composer he has never been surpassed, and of all the great music in the world it is difficult to think of any that is greater or more inspiring. His music has blessed millions of people for centuries, and it is enlightening to realize that Bach was a Christian, a Lutheran layman.

Comparing Principles

It would be incorrect to say that Christian principles and business principles are the same thing, but we can observe that there is no contradiction between them. In fact, both the business world and the church can learn from each other. Most successful businesses already practice integrity and morality in their dealings, and those who do not would find it rewarding and profitable to enhance their operations in this direction. Likewise, many large and successful churches have found it expedient to incorporate sound business practices in their operations, and this has helped them become larger and more successful. There is no question that all churches could benefit from following that example.

As an accounting professor in a secular, state-supported university, it has been my practice to lecture on professional ethics on the first day of class of every semester. Many students have the impression that, to succeed business, it is necessary to lie, cheat, and steal. This is not true and it never has been. In my lecture, I encourage the students to follow good business ethics throughout their professional lives, and I emphasize that there is never any reason to tell a lie in business. All business dealings should be completely honest, and I have never found any exceptions to this simple truth. I point out that we should go beyond ethics to what I call business morality, and that we should practice business morality in conducting all of our affairs. High level business principles should be followed in all transactions.

A question that always arose concerned the source of those high level business standards. I suggest that there are several, such as the Ten Commandments, the Golden Rule, and the Sermon on the Mount; in fact, the entire Judeo-Christian ethic. I let them know that I am a Christian and have been most of my life, and my experience is that Christian principles make fine business principles. We can follow them and enjoy great success in our chosen careers.

What Can We Conclude?

The work of God deserves the very best we have to offer. That is why we expect ministers to be graduates of Bible colleges or seminaries. Accordingly, ministers should accept no standard other than excellence. Church musicians should be highly talented and well trained. Everyone involved in church administration should look upon excellence as the norm rather than a happy accident. It follows, then, that the way the church conducts its business should be impeccable in every way. It cannot do better than to take the best practices employed in the business world and incorporate them in administering the church's business affairs.

This brings us to the purpose of this book. My hope is that it will guide pastors and their boards in installing the disciplines of internal control, accounting, finance, management, marketing, and production in doing the church's business as it fulfills the Great Commission, all of which will promote church growth. This is a worthy goal and is, I am convinced, pleasing to the Lord.

Helpful Resources
For Growing Churches
From CSS Publishing Company

Evangelism/Church Growth

Built By The Owner's Design: The Positive Approach To Building Your Church God's Way, Danny Von Kanel (2003) ISBN 0-7880-1952-X.

Grounded in solid research and Von Kanel's own experience in several growing ministries, this book outlines a proven framework for lasting growth in diverse situations. Several checklists are included to help you systematically evaluate your situation and develop a tailor-made growth plan.

Building Sunday School By The Owner's Design: 100 Tools For Successful Kingdom Growth, Danny Von Kanel (2005) ISBN 0-7880-2353-5.

A comprehensive toolbox jam-packed with ideas making Sunday school the vital centerpiece of a spiritually thriving ministry. Convenient "Tool Time" and "Tool Resource" sections offer specific steps for implementing these ideas in your church.

Get Ready ... Get Set ... GROW! Church Growth For Town And Country Congregations, Gary W. Exman (2004, revised ed.) ISBN 0-89536-865-X.

A practical handbook that demonstrates how to revitalize rural or small town congregations by applying the principles of the "church growth" movement.

It Works For Us! The Clergy's Church Growth Handbook, Michael B. Brown (1993) ISBN 1-55673-509-X.

A well-known United Methodist expert on evangelism and church growth shares a positive, biblically based program for increasing membership and attendance.

Called To Witness: A Manual For Congregational Growth, Jerry L. Schmalenberger (1993) ISBN 1-55673-558-8.

A former seminary president and parish pastor identifies three common themes for congregations seeking to grow: an emphasis on church programs, church growth methodology, and discipling.

Solving The Missing Member Puzzle, Arlon K. Stubbe (2005) ISBN 0-7880-2352-7.

Keep your "missing members" from drifting away with this book that helps you spot potential dropouts in advance, learn the reasons why they become inactive, and counteract the process with a proactive strategy for reaching them while they are still within your grasp.

Way To Grow: Dynamic Church Growth Through Small Groups, Ron Lavin (1996) ISBN 0-7880-0733-5.

This detailed discussion focuses on five different kinds of small group structures for discipleship development. By nurturing spiritual growth, small groups create a dynamic that leads to growth in numbers.

Faith Development
Questions Of Faith For Inquiring Believers, R. Robert Cueni (2002) ISBN 0-7880-1872-8.

Many people come to church today spiritually hungry but theologically uninformed. This book poses broad philosophical questions and presents open-ended and non-technical introductions to many core Christian ideas, such as atonement, ecclesiology, and prayer. An excellent resource for connecting basic theology with contemporary life.

Percolated Faith: Forming New Adult Christians Through Conversion And Baptism, Frank G. Honeycutt (1996) ISBN 0-7880-0563-4.

Honeycutt outlines a detailed program of worship, Christian education, and social outreach designed to produce authentic disciples of Christ who are more firmly rooted in their faith.

Preparation For Discipleship: A Handbook For New Christians, Jerry L. Schmalenberger (1998) ISBN 0-7880-1181-2.

Written in easy-to-understand language, this guide helps new members understand the language and rituals of the Christian faith — and what it means to be a disciple of Jesus Christ.

Stewardship

Proven Resources For Stewardship Promotion, Allan J. Weenink (2002) ISBN 0-7880-1880-9.

Developed during stewardship workshops and seminars, this book provides a wealth of proven "hands-on" resources that will help you cultivate the grace of generosity vital for Christian ministry.

From Every Angle: A Compendium Of Stewardship Resources (2000) ISBN 0-7880-1768-3.

A complete package of innovative resources for planning and executing a successful stewardship campaign: sermons, children's object lessons, insightful dramatic sketches, monthly committee agendas, a detailed advance planning guide, and much more.

A Step At A Time: Growing Givers Through Stewardship Letters, Glenn L. Borreson (2001) ISBN 0-7880-1847-7.

A practical and easy-to-follow plan for increasing congregational giving through personalized stewardship letters. This field-tested approach moves beyond mere fundraising toward developing the grace of generous giving as a mark of Christian character.

How To Talk About Money Every Sunday (Without Talking About Money), Leon Collier (2005) ISBN 0-7880-2343-8.

With this collection of brief offering sentences touching on the themes of giving, offering, and sacrifice you can instill the vital importance of generous giving in your congregation — without having to make a direct financial plea!

Mrs. Johnson's Rummage Sale And Other Stewardship Dramas, Jeff Wedge (2003) ISBN 0-7880-1971-6.

This flexible collection of seven brief sketches, each highlighting a different aspect of stewardship, is an excellent supplement to other stewardship programs. The scenes can easily be performed during the worship service, or as part of a congregational meeting, dinner, or other program.

Money And The Kingdom Of God, Maurice A. Fetty (2002) ISBN 0-7880-1903-1.

Though conventional wisdom holds that money is the "root of all evil," this book stresses that in Jesus' view, money and God's kingdom are intertwined— and that what we do with our money is indelibly linked with faithful living.

Church Administration/Management

Church Safety And Security: A Practical Guide, Robert M. Cirtin (2005) ISBN 0-7880-2341-1.

Protect your facility, staff, and worshipers with the specific proactive steps outlined in this book. Drawing on the experience of a team of professionals, it provides a wealth of practical "how-to" information on preparing for and responding to the challenges of a dangerous world.

Stay Out Of Court And Stay In Ministry, Clarance Hagglund and Britton Weimer (1998) ISBN 0-7880-1185-5.

Written to help pastors prevent costly and career-ending lawsuits, this book penned by practicing attorneys examines common real-life legal claims against religious organizations and analyzes the defenses they have raised.

Firm Foundations: An Architect And A Pastor Guide Your Church Construction, Lance Moore and Daniel Michal (1999) ISBN 0-7880-1345-9.

Many churches building or renovating repeat common mistakes — some with disastrous results. Point by point, start to finish, an architect and a pastor with experience in a wide variety of church building projects offer sage advice in sorting out the best choices for your church.

Silent Words Loudly Spoken: Church Sign Sayings, David J. Claassen (2005) ISBN 0-7880-2342-X.

Like a miniature billboard, the church sign offers a unique opportunity to share God's love — it's a powerful pulpit from which brief, but significant messages are communicated to a spiritually thirsty world. This collection of more than 700 uplifting, thought-provoking statements (conveniently formatted to easily fit most signs) helps you maximize the impact of your message board.

The Proverbial Marquee: Words To Drive By, Tina Rabb and Deborah Davies (2001) ISBN 0-7880-1801-9.

Especially developed for use with church signage, this complete collection of proven proverbs and original wisdom compiled by advertising copywriters is especially formatted for easy drive-by reading. A convenient letter count is provided for each message.